THE
COCKTAIL
BOOK

THE
COCKTAIL
BOOK

BRITISH LIBRARY

First published in 1900 by L. C. Page & Company

This edition published in 2017 by
The British Library
96 Euston Road
London NW1 2DB

British Library Cataloguing in Publication Data

A catalogue record for this book is available from the British Library

ISBN 978 0 7123 5690 9

This book has been re-typeset with minor typographical alterations

A new glossary has been added by Jon Crabb,
a writer and editor at the British Library

Designed and typeset by Tetragon, London
Printed in Malta by Gutenberg Press

To know how to drink wine belongs only to a cultivated taste; to know how to tempt guests to indulge in it with pleasure belongs only to the host gifted with rare tact and artistic discrimination.

It reminded him very much of the American cocktail. A Frenchman coming to America said that the American cocktail was a contradiction. He said, "You put a little whisky in to make it strong; you put a little water in to make it weak; you put a little lemon in to make it sour; you put a little sugar in to make it sweet, and then you say, 'Here's to you,' and you drink it yourself."

CONTENTS

Introduction

THIS BOOK is not placed before the public as a "bar-tender's guide," nor is it a list of all the fancy combinations of various liquors invented to advertise certain establishments, or for imposing on the ignorant. It is a recipe book compiled for private use. By following the directions given, it is hoped that any gentleman will be able to provide his friends with most of the standard beverages, mixed in an acceptable manner.

For the use of those who have not been in the habit of handling wines, some hints are given concerning the care, the serving, and the combining of the various kinds, so that the qualities of a good dinner will not be marred by an injudicious disposition of the liquids.

COCKTAILS

If all your beauties, one by one,
I pledge, dear, I am thinking
Before the tale were well begun
I had been dead of drinking

OLIVER HERFORD

THERE are several ways of mixing a cocktail. Some prefer to shake it thoroughly; by doing this it is made very cold. The best way to make a cocktail in a mixing glass is to stir it with a fork rather than with a spoon. By this method the ice is melted faster, cooking the liquor faster, and diluting it a little more.

It is quite customary, in serving a dry cocktail, to put an olive, preferably stoned, in the glass. With a sweeter one a maraschino cherry, or a small preserved orange is generally given.

THE TRUE STORY
OF THE COCKTAIL

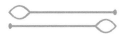

THIS is the true and delightful history of that most delicious of beverages, the "Cock's Tail"; of how it came by its name, and of the maid, Daisy Allen, who contrived it, together with sundry recipes for its making.

Now it has long been known among all those who love good liquor and a pretty face, and more particularly among the soldiers (truly most discerning and thirsty brutes), that nowhere in all the valley can be had such refreshment for man and beast as at the sign of the Bunch of Grapes, in Kingston; and that no more genial host ever beamed forth heartier comfort to the weary passengers who halted there than Squire Allen; and that no prettier maid, whether to draw a bumper or toss a kiss, stood behind the bar than the Squire's chief failing, Daisy.

Nor is it less known that, though the Squire was ever a stout fellow himself, and as quick with a buffet as any man, and as ready with a smile, he had yet another failing beside Daisy, in that he was inordinately fond of the wholesome sport of cock-fighting, and that whoso injured or even spoke an ill word of one of his birds, stood in sore danger of his hide.

So when, after an unwonted period of ill-humour and testiness, and much fidgeting of his big self about the neighbourhood, the Squire at last told dismally of the loss of his finest bird, the townsfolk knew that it would go hard with the rascal who had stolen him, and that he who was so lucky as to find and restore the bird would be welcome at the Bunch of Grapes always, no matter how many marks stood under his mug on the soapstone chimney-piece by the bar.

So for many days things went on; not even Daisy being able to cheer the heart of her father, though her own was none too light. And then, one day, came a young lieutenant riding gaily into town with the selfsame great bird under his arm. He leaped from his horse, and was seized by the Squire, so overjoyed at the return of his pet that he forgot in a moment all his ill-humour, and called for the best in the house to refresh the young man.

Now, whether it were from excitement, or nervousness, or accident, or whether, perchance, Mistress Daisy had before discovered the secret, and held it close for a great event, certain it is that she mixed sundry drops of bitters and wine of roots with a dram of good Kentucky whiskey, the whole poured over some generous bits of ice (not a little luxury in itself), and they all drank of the beverage "to the cock's tail," – for Jupiter had not lost a single feather.

And then the gallant lieutenant swore bravely that, in memory of the event, the delectable mixture he had drunk should be known through all the army as a cock's tail.

That he has been as good as his word you may all bear me witness, for who of you have not drunk the stuff, too much, perhaps, and each better than the last? But nowhere can it be had of finer quality, or smoother mix, than at the Bunch of Grapes, where the hearty lieutenant and his pretty wife, Daisy, still tell the tale, and where even the Squire – an old man now – will leave his whole yard of poultry for a cock's tail.

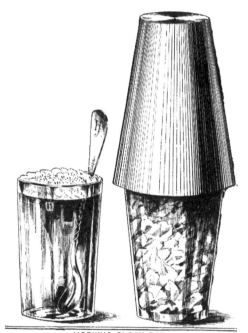

MORNING GLORY FIZZ.

Absinthe Cocktail

Use Mixing Glass

TWO dashes Angostura bitters; two dashes gum syrup; one pony absinthe. Fill with ice, mix well, and strain into a cocktail glass.

Algonquin Cocktail

Use Mixing Glass

FOUR dashes wormwood; one portion Holland gin. Fill with ice, mix, and strain into a cocktail glass.

Apple Brandy Cocktail

Use Mixing Glass

TWO dashes Boker's bitters; one portion apple brandy. Fill with ice, mix, and strain into a cocktail glass.

Armour Cocktail

Use Mixing Glass

THREE dashes orange bitters; one-half sherry and one-half vermouth. Fill with ice, mix well, and strain into a cocktail glass. Add a piece of orange peel.

Blackthorn Cocktail

Use Mixing Glass

TWO dashes orange bitters; two-thirds Tom gin; one-third Sloe gin. Fill with ice, mix, and strain into a cocktail glass.

Blenton Cocktail

Use Mixing Glass

TWO dashes orange bitters; one-half Plymouth gin; one-half French vermouth. Fill with ice, mix, and strain into a cocktail glass.

Brandy Cocktail

Use Mixing Glass

TWO dashes gum syrup; two dashes Boker's bitters; one portion brandy. Fill with ice, mix, and strain into a cocktail glass.

Brandy Cocktail — Fancy

Use Mixing Glass

THREE dashes maraschino; two dashes Boker's bitters; one dash orange bitters; one portion brandy. Fill with ice, mix, and strain into a cocktail glass, the rim of which has been moistened with a piece of lemon and dipped in powdered sugar.

Brandy Cocktail — Old-fashioned

CRUSH lump of sugar in a whiskey glass with sufficient hot water to cover the sugar. Add one lump of ice; two dashes bitters; a small piece lemon peel; one portion brandy. Stir with small bar spoon. Serve, leaving spoon in glass.

Brut Cocktail

Use Mixing Glass

THREE dashes orange bitters; one portion Italian vermouth; three dashes acid phosphate. Fill with ice, shake well, and strain into a cocktail glass.

Calisaya Cocktail

Use Mixing Glass

ONE-HALF Calisaya, one-half whiskey; one small piece lemon peel. Fill with ice, mix well, and strain into a cocktail glass.

Champagne Cocktail

Use Long, Thin Glass

ONE lump cut loaf sugar, saturated with Boker's bitters; one lump ice; one piece lemon peel. Fill glass with cold champagne, stir with spoon, and serve.

CHAMPAGNE COCKTAIL.

CHAMPAGNE SOUR.   BRANDY CRUSTA.

Cholera Cocktail

Use Bar Glass

HALF a teaspoonful Jamaica ginger; half a pony brandy; half a pony port wine; one and a half ponies cherry brandy, one and a half ponies blackberry brandy. Grate nutmeg, and stir in with spoon. Use no ice.

Chocolate Cocktail

Use Mixing Glass

ONE fresh egg; one dash bitters; one portion port wine; one teaspoonful fine sugar. Fill with ice, shake well, and strain into a cocktail glass.

Cider Cocktail

Use Thin Cider Glass

ONE lump cut loaf sugar, saturated with Boker's bitters; one lump ice; one small piece lemon peel. Fill with cold cider, stir with spoon, and serve.

Coffee Cocktail

Use Mixing Glass

ONE teaspoonful powdered sugar; one fresh egg; one portion port wine; one portion brandy. Fill with ice, shake thoroughly, and strain into a large cocktail glass. Grate a little nutmeg on top before serving.

Country Cocktail

Use Mixing Glass

TWO dashes orange bitters; two dashes Boker's bitters; one piece lemon peel; one portion rye whiskey. Fill with ice, mix well, and strain into a cocktail glass.

Deronda Cocktail

ONE-THIRD Calisaya; two-thirds Plymouth gin. Fill with ice, mix well, and strain into a cocktail glass.

Duplex Cocktail

Use Mixing Glass

THREE dashes orange bitters; one-half Italian vermouth; one-half French vermouth; three dashes acid phosphate. Fill with ice, shake well, and strain into a cocktail glass.

Florida Cocktail

Use Medium-sized Tumbler

FILL glass three-quarters with ice, juice of one lemon and one and a half oranges. Stir with spoon and serve.

Gin Cocktail — Holland

Use Mixing Glass

TWO dashes Boker's bitters; two dashes gum syrup; one portion Holland gin. Fill with ice, mix, and strain into a cocktail glass.

Gin Cocktail — Old-fashioned Holland

PUT a lump of sugar in a whiskey glass, and cover it with hot water. Crush the sugar; add lump of ice, two dashes Boker's bitters, small piece lemon peel, one portion Holland gin. Mix with small bar spoon, and serve with spoon in glass.

Gin Cocktail — Plymouth

Use Mixing Glass

THREE dashes orange bitters; one portion Plymouth gin. Fill with ice, mix well, and strain into a cocktail glass.

Gin Cocktail — Tom

Use Mixing Glass

TWO dashes orange or Boker's bitters; one portion Tom gin. Fill with ice, mix, and strain into a cocktail glass.

Gin Cocktail — Old-fashioned Tom

MAKE the same as an Old-fashioned Holland Gin Cocktail, using Tom in the place of Holland gin.

Harvard Cocktail

Use Mixing Glass

ONE dash gum syrup; three dashes Boker's bitters; one-half Italian vermouth; one-half brandy. Fill with ice, mix, and strain into a cocktail glass, then fill with seltzer and serve quickly.

Irish Cocktail

Use Mixing Glass

THREE dashes orange bitters; two dashes Horsford's acid phosphate; one-half Italian vermouth; one-half whiskey. Fill with ice, mix, and strain into a cocktail glass.

Jamaica Rum Cocktail

Use Mixing Glass

TWO dashes gum syrup; two dashes orange bitters; two dashes Boker's bitters; one portion Jamaica rum. Fill with ice, mix, and strain into a cocktail glass.

Jersey Cocktail

Use Thin Cider Glass

ONE lump ice; one-half teaspoonful fine sugar; two dashes Boker's bitters; one piece lemon peel. Fill up with cold cider. Stir well, and serve while effervescent.

Lemon Cocktail

Use Mixing Glass

TWO dashes Angostura bitters; two dashes gum syrup; lemon juice. Fill with ice, mix, and strain into a cocktail glass.

Liberal Cocktail

Use Mixing Glass

ONE dash syrup; half Picon bitters; one-half whiskey. Fill with ice, mix, strain into a cocktail glass, and put a small piece of lemon peel on top.

Lone Tree Cocktail

ONE-HALF Italian vermouth; one-half Tom gin. No bitters. Fill with ice, mix, and strain into a cocktail glass.

Manhattan Cocktail

Use Mixing Glass

TWO dashes gum syrup; two dashes Boker's bitters; one-half Italian vermouth; one-half whiskey. Fill with ice, mix, and strain. Add a small twist of lemon peel.

Manhattan Cocktail — Dry

MAKE the same as a Manhattan cocktail, leaving out the syrup.

Manhattan Cocktail — Extra Dry

MAKE the same as the dry cocktail, using French vermouth instead of Italian.

Martini Cocktail — No. 1

Use Mixing Glass

THREE dashes orange bitters; one-half Tom gin; one-half Italian vermouth; small piece lemon peel. Fill with ice, mix, and strain into a cocktail glass.

Martini Cocktail — No. 2

Use Mixing Glass

TWO dashes Boker's bitters; one-half Tom gin; one-half Italian vermouth; half a teaspoonful sherry, small piece lemon peel. Fill with ice, mix, and strain into a cocktail glass.

MEDFORD RUM COCKTAIL

Use Mixing Glass

ONE dash gum syrup; two dashes Boker's bitters; one portion Medford rum. Fill with ice, mix, and strain into a cocktail glass.

METROPOLE COCKTAIL

Use Mixing Glass

TWO dashes gum syrup; two dashes Peyschaud bitters; one dash orange bitters; one-half brandy; one-half French vermouth. Fill with ice, mix, and strain into a cocktail glass.

NARRAGANSETT COCKTAIL

Use Mixing Glass

TWO-THIRDS whiskey; one-third Italian vermouth; one dash absinthe. No bitters. Fill with ice, mix, and strain into a cocktail glass.

New Orleans Cocktail

Use Mixing Glass

ONE dash Angostura bitters; one portion Italian vermouth. Fill with ice, shake well, strain into a star champagne glass. Fill with soda water.

Oyster Cocktail

Use Tumbler

A few dashes lemon juice; one dash Tobasco sauce; one teaspoonful vinegar; a few dashes tomato catsup; six oysters with all their liquor. Season to taste with pepper and salt. Mix, and serve with small fork in the glass.

Princeton Cocktail

Use Mixing Glass

THREE dashes orange bitters; three-quarters Tom gin. Fill with ice, mix, and strain into a cocktail glass. Add one-quarter port wine carefully, and let it settle to bottom before serving.

Puritan Cocktail

Use Mixing Glass

THREE dashes orange bitters; one spoonful yellow chartreuse; two-thirds Plymouth gin; one-third French vermouth. Fill with ice, mix, and strain into a cocktail glass.

Riding Club Cocktail

Use Mixing Glass

ONE glass Angostura bitters; small spoonful Horsford's acid phosphate; one portion Calisaya. Fill with ice, mix, and strain into a cocktail glass.

Rob Roy Cocktail

Use Mixing Glass

TWO dashes orange bitters; two-thirds Scotch whiskey; one-third Italian vermouth. Fill with ice, mix, and strain into a cocktail glass. Serve an olive in the glass.

Soda Cocktail

Use Large Glass

THREE or four lumps of ice; one teaspoonful powdered sugar; three dashes Angostura or Boker's bitters; one bottle plain soda, or lemon soda; one slice lemon peel. Stir with spoon and serve. In mixing, care should be taken that the soda does not run over the glass.

Star Cocktail

Use Mixing Glass

TWO dashes gum syrup; three dashes orange bitters; one-half apple brandy; one-half Italian vermouth. Fill with ice, mix, strain into a cocktail glass, and add small twist of lemon peel.

Thistle Cocktail

Use Mixing Glass

TWO dashes Angostura bitters; one-third Italian vermouth; two-thirds Scotch whiskey. Fill with ice, mix, and strain into a cocktail glass. Add curl of lemon peel.

Trilby Cocktail

Use Mixing Glass

THREE dashes orange bitters; three dashes acid phosphate; two-thirds whiskey; one-third Calisaya. Fill with ice, mix, and strain into a cocktail glass.

Turf Cocktail

Use Mixing Glass

TWO dashes Angostura bitters; one-half Tom gin; one-half Italian vermouth. Fill glass with ice, stir well, and strain into a cocktail glass.

Tuxedo Cocktail

Use Mixing Glass

ONE dash Angostura bitters; one spoonful sherry; one-half Tom gin; one-half Italian vermouth. Fill with ice, mix, and strain into a cocktail glass.

Vermouth Cocktail

Use Mixing Glass

TWO dashes Boker's or Peyschaud bitters; one portion Italian vermouth. Fill with ice, mix, and strain into a cocktail glass.

Vermouth Cocktail — Dry

MAKE the same as Vermouth Cocktail, substituting French vermouth for Italian.

Vermouth Cocktail — Fancy

Use Mixing Glass

THREE dashes maraschino, two dashes Boker's bitters; one portion Italian vermouth; one dash orange bitters. Fill with ice, mix, and strain into a cocktail glass, the rim of which has been moistened with a piece of lemon peel and dipped into powdered sugar.

Vermouth Cocktail — French

Use Mixing Glass

THREE dashes orange bitters; one portion French vermouth. Fill with ice, mix, and strain into a cocktail glass.

Whiskey Cocktail

Use Mixing Glass

TWO dashes gum syrup; two dashes Peyschaud bitters; one portion whiskey. Fill with ice, mix, and strain into a cocktail glass. Add a twist of lemon peel.

Whiskey Cocktail — Fancy

Use Mixing Glass

TWO dashes maraschino; two dashes Boker's bitters; one dash orange bitters; one portion whiskey. Fill with ice and mix till very cold. Strain into a cocktail glass, the rim of which has been moistened with lemon juice and dipped into powdered sugar.

Whiskey Cocktail — New York

Use Mixing Glass

T W O dashes Boker's bitters; one-half whiskey; one-half Italian vermouth; half a teaspoonful sherry. Fill with ice, mix, and strain into a cocktail glass. Add small piece lemon peel.

Whiskey Cocktail — Old-fashioned

P U T a lump of sugar in a whiskey glass; add enough hot water to cover the sugar. Crush the sugar; add a lump of ice, two dashes Boker's bitters, one portion whiskey, small piece lemon peel. Mix with small spoon, and serve with spoon in glass.

Yale Cocktail

Use Mixing Glass

T H R E E dashes orange bitters; one dash Boker's bitters; piece lemon peel; one portion Tom gin. Fill with ice, mix, and strain into a cocktail glass; add a squirt of siphon seltzer.

York Cocktail

Use Mixing Glass

ONE dash Boker's bitters; two dashes orange bitters; two-thirds Scotch whiskey; one-third Italian vermouth. Fill with ice, mix, and strain into a cocktail glass.

MISCELLANEOUS
MIXED DRINKS

Fill up the bowl; upon my soul,
Your trouble you'll forget, sir.
If it takes more, fill twenty score,
Till you have drowned regret, sir.

Absinthe Frappé

Use Mixing Glass

ONE pony absinthe. Fill glass with fine ice, shake well, and strain into a cocktail glass.

Brandy Flip

ONE teaspoonful sugar; one wine glass brandy; one fresh egg. Fill glass half full of fine shaved ice. Shake well in shaker. Strain into star champagne glass, and grate a little nutmeg on top.

Brandy Smash

Use Mixing Glass

HALF tablespoonful sugar; half wine glass water; dissolve; three or four sprigs fresh mint; half glass fine shaved ice; one wine glass brandy. Stir well with spoon. Strain into fancy bar glass, and ornament with fruit in season.

Brooklyn Kümmel

Use Cocktail Glass

FILL glass with fine shaved ice, place on top a slice of lemon. Pour the kümmel over this until the glass is full.

Buttered Rum

Use Tumbler

ONE lump sugar; dissolve in hot water; one-third rum; two-thirds hot water; butter the size of a walnut. Grate a little nutmeg on top.

Café Kirsch

Use Mixing Glass

FILL glass half full of fine ice; half a cup of hot black coffee; one pony Kirschwasser. Shake, and strain into a cocktail glass.

California Absinthe

Use Mixing Glass

ONE pony absinthe. Fill glass with fine ice. Shake well, strain into star champagne glass, and fill with siphon.

Champagne Cobbler

Use Delicate Wine Glass

SMALL lump sugar. Fill glass with shaved ice. Pour in champagne till the glass is full. Serve with straw, and decorate with fruit and leaves.

Champagne Cup

Use Glass Pitcher

HALF tablespoonful sugar; one rind of lemon; three slices orange; three slices lemon; berries; one slice cucumber peel; one pony brandy; one pony maraschino; one pony white curaçao; one wine glass sherry; one quart champagne; one bottle soda; two or three large lumps of ice. Ornament with fresh mint.

Cider Cup

SAME as Champagne Cup, using cider in the place of champagne.

Claret Cobbler

Use Large Glass

ONE tablespoonful powdered sugar. Fill glass with shaved ice. Pour full of claret. Shake in shaker. Ornament with fruit and serve with straws.

Claret Cup

SAME as Champagne Cup, using claret in the place of champagne.

Claret Punch

Use Large Glass

ONE tablespoonful powdered sugar; two dashes lemon juice. Fill glass with shaved ice. Fill with claret. Shake well. Ornament with fruit, serve with straws.

Egg Nog

Use Mixing Glass

THREE-QUARTERS tablespoon sugar; one wine glass whiskey or brandy; one-half glass shaved ice; one fresh egg. Fill glass with fresh milk. Shake well, strain into a large glass, and grate over it a little nutmeg.

Bowl of Egg Nog

SUITABLE FOR NEW YEAR'S PARTY

This recipe is for making a two-gallon bowl full

TWO pounds fine powdered sugar; twenty fresh eggs. Have the yolks separated and beaten till thin as water. Add the yolks to the sugar, and dissolve well with spoon. Two quarts good old brandy; one and a half pints St. Croix or Jamaica rum; one and a half gallons rich milk. Mix the ingredients well with ladle, stirring continually while pouring in the milk. Beat the whites of eggs to stiff froth. Pour this froth carefully over the mixture. In serving, dip out with ladle. Put a little of the white on the top of each help, and grate on a little nutmeg. Serve in punch glasses.

Gin Fizz

Use Mixing Glass

ONE-HALF tablespoonful sugar; three or four dashes lemon juice; one wine glass Tom gin. Fill glass with ice; shake; strain into fizz glass, and fill up with soda.

Gin Rickey

Use Medium-sized Tumbler

JUICE one lime; leave half of the pressed lime in glass; one lump ice; one wine glass Tom gin. Fill with siphon.

Golden Fizz

Use Mixing Glass

ONE-HALF tablespoonful sugar; three or four dashes lemon juice; one wine glass Tom gin; yolk of one egg. Fill glass with ice, shake well, and strain into fizz glass. Fill with siphon.

Hot Applejack

Use Hot Water Glass

TWO lumps sugar. Fill glass two-thirds full of boiling water and dissolve sugar. One wine glass applejack; one slice lemon. Serve with spoon.

Hot Apple Toddy

Use Hot Water Glass

HALF tablespoonful sugar. Fill glass two-thirds with boiling water. One wine glass applejack; two spoonfuls baked apple. Grate over a little nutmeg, and serve with spoon.

Hot Irish

TWO lumps sugar. Fill glass two-thirds with boiling water; dissolve sugar. One wine glass full Irish whiskey; one slice lemon peel. Serve with spoon.

Hot Scotch

Use Hot Water Glass

TWO lumps sugar. Fill glass two-thirds full boiling water, and dissolve sugar. One wine glass Scotch whiskey; one slice lemon peel. Serve with spoon.

Hot Spiced Rum

Use Hot Water Glass

ONE or two lumps loaf sugar. Fill glass two-thirds full boiling water, and dissolve sugar; one wine glass Jamaica rum; six or eight cloves. Serve with spoon. Good for sore throat.

John Collins

Use Long Glass

ONE-HALF teaspoonful sugar; five or six dashes lemon juice; one wine glass Holland gin. Dissolve the sugar with spoon; add three or four lumps of ice, and pour in a bottle of soda water.

ST. CHARLES PUNCH.   BRANDY PUNCH.

MINT JULEP.

Medford Rum Punch

Use Large Glass

THREE-QUARTERS tablespoonful powdered sugar; two or three dashes lemon juice. Dissolve with a little water. Fill glass with fine shaved ice. One and a quarter wine glass Medford rum. Shake well, and ornament with fruit. Serve with straws.

Milk Punch

Use Mixing Glass

THREE-QUARTERS tablespoonful sugar; one wine glass whiskey or brandy; one-half glass shaved ice. Fill glass with good milk, shake, and strain into large glass. Grate a little nutmeg on top.

Mint Julep

ONE-HALF tablespoonful sugar; one-half wine glass water; three or four sprigs fresh mint. Stir well till the essence of mint is well extracted. Fill up glass with shaved ice. One wine glass whiskey or brandy. Shake well and ornament with fruit and mint-leaves.

Pink One

Use Mixing Glass

THREE or four dashes lemon juice; one wine glass Tom gin; one-half pony Grenadine. Shake, strain into fizz glass, and fill with siphon.

Plush

Use Glass Pitcher

TWO or three large lumps ice; one pint champagne; one pint claret. Pour into pitcher and stir with spoon.

Port and Starboard

Use Pousse Café Glass

ONE-HALF orange curaçao; one-half green mint. Pour carefully so that they will not mix.

Port Wine Flip

Use Mixing Glass

ONE teaspoonful powdered sugar; one wine glass port wine; one fresh egg. Fill glass half full of shaved ice. Shake well, strain into star champagne glass, and grate a little nutmeg on top.

Port Wine Sangaree

Use Mixing Glass

ONE teaspoonful sugar dissolved in a little water; one wine glass port wine; five or six lumps of ice. Stir with spoon. Strain into a star champagne glass, and grate a little nutmeg on top.

Pousse Café

Use Pousse Café Glass

ONE-SIXTH each of the following: Raspberry syrup, maraschino, orange curaçao, yellow Chartreuse, green Chartreuse, and brandy. Pour in carefully so that they will not mix.

Pousse L'Amour

Use Sherry Glass

ONE-QUARTER sherry glass maraschino; yolk of egg, cold; quarter of a glass of vanilla; quarter of a glass of cognac. Take great care that the egg does not mix with the cordials.

Remsen Cooler

Use Large Glass

ONE whole rind of lemon; three lumps of ice; one portion Tom gin; one bottle plain soda.

Rhine Wine Cobbler

ONE tablespoonful powdered sugar; one-half glass water. Dissolve well with spoon. Fill glass with shaved ice. Fill with Rhine wine. Shake well and ornament with fruits. Serve with straws.

Rickety Scotch

Use Medium-sized Tumbler

HALF a lime squeezed into glass; two dashes lemon juice; one wine glass Scotch whiskey; one lump ice. Fill with siphon.

Royal Plush

Use Glass Pitcher

TWO or three large lumps ice; one pint champagne; one pint of Burgundy. Pour into glass pitcher and stir with spoon.

Sam Ward

RIND of one lemon placed in cocktail glass; fill with fine ice; then fill the glass with yellow Chartreuse.

Sauterne Cobbler

Use Large Glass

THREE-QUARTERS tablespoonful powdered sugar; one-quarter wine glass water. Dissolve well with spoon. Fill glass with fine shaved ice; one and a half wine glassfuls sauterne. Shake well and ornament with fruit. Serve with straws.

Sauterne or Hock Cup

Use Glass Pitcher

ONE tablespoonful sugar; rind of one lemon; three slices orange; three slices lemon; berries; one slice cucumber peel; one pony brandy; one pony maraschino; one wine glass sherry; one quart sauterne or hock; one bottle soda; two or three lumps ice. Ornament with fresh mint.

Shandy Gaff

Use Large Glass

HALF beer or ale; half ginger ale. This is best if the parts are poured in together.

SHERRY COBBLER

Use Large Glass

ONE tablespoonful powdered sugar dissolved in a little water. Fill glass with shaved ice. Fill with sherry; shake well. Ornament with fruits and serve with straws.

SHERRY FLIP

Use Mixing Glass

ONE teaspoonful powdered sugar; one wine glass sherry wine; one fresh egg. Fill glass half full shaved ice. Shake well; strain into star champagne glass and grate a little nutmeg on top.

SILVER FIZZ

Use Mixing Glass

ONE tablespoonful sugar; three or four dashes lemon juice; one wine glass Tom gin; white of one egg. Fill glass with ice, shake well, strain into fizz glass, and fill with siphon.

St. Croix Rum Sour

Use Mixing Glass

HALF tablespoonful sugar; two or three dashes lemon juice; one squirt of seltzer. Dissolve well. One wine glass St. Croix rum. Fill glass with ice, stir well, and strain into sour glass. Ornament with fruit.

Syracuse Cooler

RIND of whole lemon, three lumps ice; one portion Medford rum; one bottle ginger ale.

Tom Collins

Use Large Glass

MAKE same as John Collins, using Tom gin instead of Holland.

Whiskey Rickey

SAME as gin rickey, using whiskey in place of gin.

Whiskey Sour

SAME as St. Croix Rum Sour, using whiskey in place of rum.

NON-ALCOHOLIC DRINKS

Here's lovers two to the maiden true,
And four to the maid caressing,
But the wayward girl, with the lips that curl,
Keeps twenty lovers guessing.

Boston Cooler

Use Large Glass

RIND of one lemon; three lumps ice; bottle sarsaparilla; bottle ginger ale.

Brunswick

Use Mixing Glass

HALF tablespoonful sugar; one fresh egg; half glass shaved ice. Fill glass with ice, shake, strain into large glass, and grate nutmeg on top. Serve with straws.

Bull's Eye

Use Large Glass

RIND of one lemon; three lumps ice; half pint cider; one bottle ginger ale.

Horse's Neck

Use Large Glass

RIND one lemon; two or three lumps ice; one bottle ginger ale. Stir with spoon.

Lemonade

Use Large Glass

TABLESPOONFUL sugar; three or four dashes lemon juice; three or four lumps ice. Fill glass with water, shake well, and ornament with fruits. Serve with straws.

Egg Lemonade

Use Mixing Glass

ONE fresh egg; tablespoonful sugar; four or five dashes lemon juice; four or five lumps ice. Fill with water, shake well, and strain into a large glass.

Soda Lemonade

Use Large Glass

TABLESPOONFUL sugar; three or four dashes lemon juice; three or four lumps ice; bottle plain soda. Stir well with spoon, remove ice and serve.

Limeade

Use Large Glass

TABLESPOONFUL sugar; juice three limes. Fill glass half full shaved ice. Fill with water, shake well, and dress with fruit. Serve with straws.

Mule's Collar

Use Large Glass

JUICE one lime; one dash Angostura bitters; three lumps ice; one bottle dry ginger ale.

Orangeade

Use Large Glass

TABLESPOONFUL sugar. Squeeze the juice of one orange. Fill glass half full with fine shaved ice. Fill with water, shake well, and dress with fruit. Serve with straws.

CARE AND
SERVING
OF WINES

O little fishes of the sea,
Had I the power divine,
I'd turn you into silver cups
And your sea to purple wine.

W INE does not differ from any other luxury in this world. Each person has his own ideas and tastes concerning it. On this account, no hard and fast rules can be laid down. There are, however, certain customs which have been almost universally adopted by "good livers." These will be embodied in the following few lines.

As relating to beer or wine in the cask, it is not necessary to give any instructions. Beer served from the keg is an article scarcely ever seen in the household. If one has wine in the barrel, he must have a professional to bottle it, who is an expert at the business.

Beer or ale should not be served too cold. It may be placed near the ice, with the bottle in an upright position. It should not come in contact with the ice, as it would be chilled. In pouring it, care should be taken not to shake the bottle, so as to stir up the sediment.

Claret, Burgundy, Sauterne, hock, port, sherry, and other light wines, should always be kept with the bottle in a horizontal position. They should be served at a temperature of 60°–70°, great care being taken not to disturb the dregs.

Champagne should always be kept on its side. It should be served as cold as is possible. When it is put on the ice care should be taken not to soak off the labels, and no more should be cooled than is to be used, as it detracts from its vitality to chill and then warm it. If one has to cool champagne in a hurry, it can be well done by turning the bottle in an ice-cream freezer packed with ice and salt.

Cordials can be kept at any moderate temperature, and, like any other sweet substances, they should be protected from the invasion of insects.

Liquors, such as rum, whiskey, brandy, and gin, are generally bought in bulk, and need very little care. They are generally kept in a decanter, and served directly from the same; if any particular temperature is desired, it is regulated by the addition of hot or cold water. If liquor is to be kept a great number of years it should be bottled, the bottles laid in a horizontal position, and recorked from time to time.

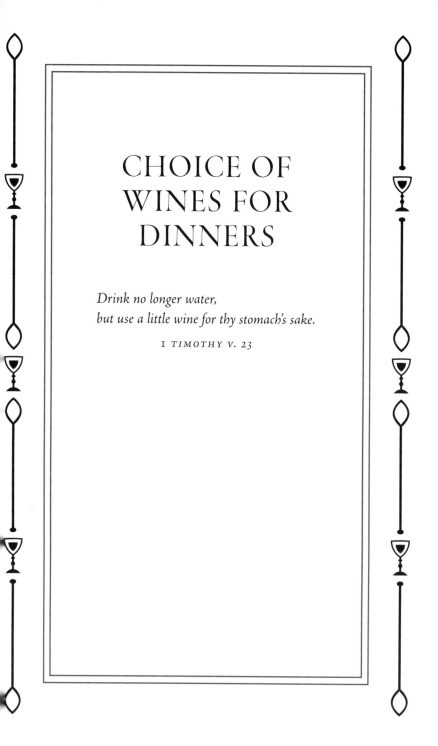

CHOICE OF WINES FOR DINNERS

Drink no longer water,
but use a little wine for thy stomach's sake.

I TIMOTHY V. 23

T HE variety of wines to be served with a dinner depends largely on the rest of the menu.

Before a stag dinner of any kind, it is generally customary to serve either a cocktail, or a glass of sherry with a dash of bitters in it. When ladies are present this is generally dispensed with.

For a small dinner of four or five courses, it is generally good form to serve sherry with the soup and fish, followed by a Sauterne, hock, or Rhine wine, and nothing further.

At very elaborate feasts the number of wines introduced is almost unlimited; but the following list is believed to contain the essential features:

With soup, sherry; with fish, white wine; with meats, Burgundy and Roman or kirsch punch; with roast meats or poultry, champagne; with entrées, champagne; with game and salads, champagne, or particularly rich claret or Burgundy; with dessert and coffee, a little burnt brandy is the most correct liquor, although any kind of cordial is largely served. The chief principle to be followed is that the choicer and heavier wines should follow the lighter ones.

THE END

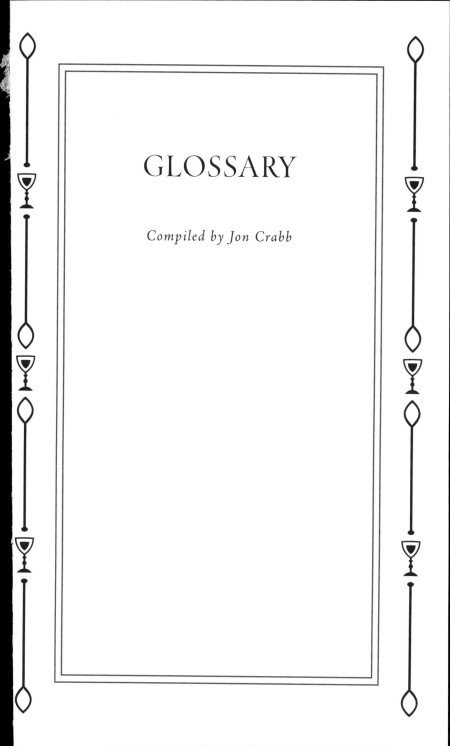

GLOSSARY

Compiled by Jon Crabb

Acid phosphate

An ingredient that went from ubiquitous to forgotten over the course of a century. Acid phosphate creates a tart, sour, yet essentially neutral, taste. Whereas lemon or lime create the same sensation but add a citrus tang, acid phosphate makes your tongue tingle without altering the flavour profile. The other flavours are in fact subtly enhanced.

Angostura Bitters

Angostura has been distilled and sold since 1824 and is one of the most popular and versatile bitters. Gentian is a primary flavour but the exact recipe is a closely guarded secret known by only five people.

Boker's Bitters

John G. Boker created this bitters in 1828 and it was one of the most common ingredients used in cocktails until the turn of the century, although it disappeared completely during the Prohibition. Interestingly, in 2009, a facsimile was created by Adam Elmegirab based on the chemical analysis of a tiny stock of original samples. This recreated Boker's Bitters can be bought through his website.

Calisaya

A generic name for a bitter herbal liquor made with cinchona bark (from which quinine is derived), bitter orange, and various other botanicals. It is a form of Italian *amaro*, and was a popular ingredient in cocktails around the turn of the century, although it disappeared from the US market after Prohibition. Cinchona-based liquors are still popular in Italy under the name china (pronounced 'keena'), the Italian name for cinchona. There is now a calisaya distilled in small batches in the United States that has trademarked the name Calisaya, but there is no reason why a reasonable approximation of a Calisaya Cocktail could not be made with any number of Italian chinas, such as China Martini.

Cut loaf sugar

A sugarloaf is a large, conical mass of hard refined sugar, and the usual form in which refined sugar was produced and sold until the late nineteenth century. One lump can be substituted for one cube, or one teaspoon of granulated sugar.

Gum syrup

A mixture of simple syrup and gum Arabic, which, when added to drinks, produces a silkier texture than simple syrup. Easy to make and worth doing.

Holland gin

Jenever, the robust ancestor of modern gin. EU regulations specify that only juniper-flavoured liquor made in the Netherlands, Belgium, two northern French departments and two German federal states can use the name. Further regulations tightly control exactly what constitutes traditional jenever.

Jamaica Ginger

A nineteenth-century patent medicine containing ginger solids dissolved in ethanol. This provided a convenient way to bypass Prohibition laws, and the 'medicine' was drunk by many poor Southerners for recreational purposes. Unfortunately for them, bootleggers adulterated some of the 'jake' supply in 1930 with an industrial plasticizer called TOCP: a potent neurotoxin that causes paralysis. Some 30,000 people lost partial use of their limbs, sometimes permanently. High-alcohol ginger extracts are hard to come by these days but you could try making your own by macerating ginger root in vodka.

Kirschwasser

Clear cherry brandy popular in Germany and Switzerland, traditionally made from a double distillation of morello cherries. The word literally means 'cherry water' in German.

Kümmel

A sweet, caraway-flavoured liqueur. It is primarily distilled and drunk in Germany, the Baltic States and Russia, although there is also a custom of drinking it in British Gentleman's Clubs and some of the more traditional golf courses. Kümmel means caraway in German, although the best versions have a complex flavour resulting from a blend of caraway, cumin, fennel and anise.

Medford rum

Medford rum was distilled by the Lawrence family in Medford, Massachusetts throughout the nineteenth century. In 1905, they closed down and sold the rights to the name. GrandTen distilling in Boston now honour the original with their own 'Medford Rum', but this is not the same drink and is made to a different recipe, in different stills, in a different town.

Peychaud's Bitters

Peychaud's Bitters was originally created around 1830 by Antoine Amédée Peychaud, a New Orleans apothecary of Haitian origin. It is gentian-based, like Angostura bitters, but slightly sweeter and fruiter. Peychaud's Bitters is manufactured by the Sazerac Company and is an essential component of the Sazerac cocktail.

Picon bitters

A bittersweet French *amer* made with fresh orange, gentian and quinquina (fortified wine containing quinine), blended with sugar, syrup and caramel. Picon was originally 39% ABV, although the strength was reduced in the 1970s and further in the 1980s to just 18%. No longer available in its original form, there are now two main products that share its name: Picon Bière, which is added to beer and remains popular in Northern France, and the slightly stronger Picon Club (21%), intended for cocktails or wine. Picon is near impossible to buy outside of France and Belgium and is not exactly the same bitters mentioned in *The Cocktail Book* anyway. There are, however, several Italian amaros based on oranges, so this route provides an alternative option for experimental enthusiasts keen to recreate classic Picon cocktails.

Plymouth gin

Gin distilled in Plymouth, England. The Plymouth Gin Distillery has been distilling the drink since 1793. Plymouth gin was the official drink of the British Royal Navy, who spread it around the world and created the Gin and Tonic in the process. In the late nineteenth century it was the world's most popular gin and a common fixture in early cocktail books.

Pony

For all intents and purposes, a 'pony' refers to a single measure or the smaller side of a bar jigger. In the United States at least, this equals 1 fluid ounce or 29.57ml. In the UK, the standard measure of a single shot is either 25ml or 35ml. A pony is also roughly equivalent to 2 tablespoons.

Sarsaparilla

A soft drink originally made from the native Central American plant *Smilax ornata*. Associated with the American Old West, sarsaparilla was popular in the United States in the nineteenth century. Sarsaparilla is now generally made with artificial flavours but the genuine article can still be found from specialist retailers.

Tom gin

Slightly sweeter than standard London dry gin, with a gentler flavour created by fewer botanicals. This forgotten style of gin sits somewhere between a jenever and a modern London dry, and is returning to popularity thanks to the craft cocktail movement.

Wormwood

The Algonquin Cocktail on p. 19 calls for 'four dashes wormwood'. If taken to mean essential oil of wormwood, this seems like a hardy move certain to produce regret. Wormwood is astonishingly and persistently bitter. For experimental purposes I once tested a drop of pure wormwood oil on my tongue and the overwhelming aftertaste lingered for hours, failing to be masked even by lunch and a coffee. I suggest that in *The Cocktail Book*, 'four dashes wormwood' refers to wormwood bitters; niche bitters that combine the enormously bitter wormwood with other botanicals to make something slightly less aggressive. A few specialist retailers sell this most bitter of bitters.